HUANGSHAN MOUNTAINS

CHINA TRAVEL AND TOURISM PRESS

Advisor: Ji Jiahong   Zhang Maixian
Chief Editor: Zhang Xiqin
Vice Chief Editor: Li Zeru   Dong Ruicheng
Designing Editor: Dong Ruicheng
Chinese Writer: Fang Junmo
Chinese Editor: Fan Yunxing
Photographer: Wang Tianbao   Wang Hongyi   Lu Daqian   Zhu Yunfeng   Zhu Tao
　　　　　　 Jiang Yaoping   Wang Ruwei   Wang Genhua   Wang Yang
　　　　　　 Li Jianzhong   Li Changjie   Gu Weiheng   Wu Zhengxun
　　　　　　 Wu Xiangdong   Wu Guangmin   Fan Guoan   Hu Guoxin
　　　　　　 Jiang Yan   Chen Donglin   Chen Suwei   Chen Mouquan   Ling Jun
　　　　　　 Ma Zhaoyun   Lu Kaiti   Yuan Lianmin   Xu Zhenshi   Huang Yongxiang
　　　　　　 Zhang Jinfu   Cheng Datong   Dong Qing   Dong Ruicheng
　　　　　　 Ye Xiaonian   Yang Zhongjian   Yang Guanghua   Meng Zi
　　　　　　 Zhao Lingsheng   Zheng Changyi   Yue Jinlin   Liu Jianping
　　　　　　 Liu Chuanyan   Xie Feng   Gu Jian
Photo Editor: Ling Jun   Dong Ruicheng
Map Drawer: Sun Suju
Map Editor: Teng Yifang
English Translator: Chen Mingming   Meng Xianyu
Foreign Language Editor: Meng Xianyu
Technology Editor: Wang Ce

CONTENTS

Heaven-Bestowed Scenery

Huangshan (the Yellow Mountains) in China's eastern Anhui Province are like a glittering green leaf viewed from an earth satellite high up in the sky; the Yellow Mountains are like a cluster of large, purple Spring Heralding Flowers in full bloom seen by tourists on the surface of the earth.

They are not only mountains, but also a sea. A sea of mountain peaks, a sea of clouds, a sea of pine trees, a sea of flowers, a sea of light, a sea of poetry. It is a sea of paintings. No wonder, the mountains have also been called the Yellow Sea (Huanghai).

Beautiful are the mountains: they constantly changd their appearance, graceful, wondrous, forever fresh and unconventional. There stand the towering peaks, but in an instant they will turn into islands above a sea of clouds, and the pine trees growing out of the crevices will look as if they had taken root in the clouds, reminding the tourists of the "jade foliage on golden branches" in the legend. As the year passes from one season to another, as the weather changes from rain to shine, as the sun sets and the moon rises, the mountain changes, continually taking on new looks. Even if you visit The Yellow Mountains a thousand times, each time you will discover new beauties and enjoy new experiences.

Beautiful are the mountains: they combine the real and the unreal. The peaks, rocks, pine trees, waterfalls and springs all bear descriptive names. The peaks are called by such names as Lianhua (Lotus), Tiandu (Celestial Capital), Yuping (Jade Screen) and Jiulong (Nine Dragons);the rocks by such names as "Golden Cock Crowing towards Heavenly Gate", "Squirrel Skipping to Celestial Capital", "Monkey Gazing at the Sea" and "Magpie on a Plum Tree"; the pine trees by such names as Yingke (Greeting Guests), Tanhai

(Probe the Sea), Heihu (Black Tiger) and Wolong (Recumbent Dragon); and the waterfalls and springs by such names as the Jiulong (Nine Dragons) Waterfall, the Renzi (Inverted-V) Waterfall, the Baizhang (Thousand Feet) Spring and the Mingxian (Ringing String) Spring. If you compare these fancy names with what you see, you may find that they do not really match. But, set off by the mist and tinted by light, these scenic spots, seen from the right angle, will look more real than what their names signify. They will be more lifelike and more fascinating. The Lianhua Peak will be a lotus flower rowing out of the clouds high up in the sky. The golden cock will be ready to fly towards the gate leading to Celestial Capital. The pine tree by the name of "Yingke" will be extending its arms to welcome guests from afar. And the stone lute beneath the Mingxian Spring will send out enchanting melodies.

Beautiful are the mountains: though old, not old, they are eternally youthful. Resulting from cataclysmic crust movement about 100 million years ago and named Yishan in the ancient Qin Dynasty (221-207 B.C.) and later renamed the Yellow Mountains in the Tang Dynasty (618-907 A.D.), the mountains are very old indeed. Yet they are young and graceful. Not relying on artificial decorations, the scenery is simple and natural, manifesting youthful vigour and heroic grandeur. The peaks here vie with one another in thrusting into the sky. The rocks here vie with one another in being grotesque. The pine trees here compete with one another in elegance. The flying clouds here link up the mountain and the sky. The hot springs here, forever bubbling, give mankind an endless flow of warmth and fervour. Even the Magua trees that have come down from glacier periods put forth new leaves every spring, looking so beautiful and so young.

1. Fairyland on Earth

2. The Sun Rising from the Sea of Clouds

5. Watching the Sea of Clouds on the
   Alchemy Peak

The Yellow Mountains - a Marvel of Natural Beauty

Located in the southern part of Anhui Province, the Yellow Mountains extend across four counties - Shexian, Yixian, Taiping and Xiuning. They rose above the earth surface as a result of movement of the earth's crust over a hundred million years ago. Later they underwent the erosion of Quaternary glaciation and have gradually become what they are today. Magnificent and imposing, it is a famous scenic spot full of wonderful sights.

The Yellow Mountains, known as Yishan in the Qin Dynasty (221-207 B.C.) got their present name in 747 A.D. (the 6th year of the Tianbao reign of the Tang Dynasty), when Li Bai (701-762), the great Tang poet, wrote about them in these lines:

Thousands of feet high towers the Yellow Mountains
With its thirty-two magnificent peaks,
Blooming like golden lotus flowers,
Amidst red crags and rock columns.

The Yellow Mountains are a marvel: within an area of 154 square kilometres there is a crowd of peaks, 72 of which have names indicating the shapes they resemble. Lotus, Brightness Apex and Celestial Capital are the three major ones, all rising above 1,800 metres. The mountains are a body of granite, often with vertical joints. Erosion and fracture contributed to shape the rocks into huge columns, giving rise to lofty peaks and deep ravines. When it is cloudy the pinnacles loom in mists as if they were visionary, while in sunshine they unfold in all their majesty and splendour. The Yellow Mountains change their colour and appearance with the alternation of seasons. In spring blooming flowers decorate the slopes in a riot of colour and fill the valleys with fragrance; in summer you see verdured peaks rising one upon another and hear springs gurgling merrily. Autumn dresses the mountains in red and purple as maples are all blazing-red; winter turns them into a world of frost and ice with silver boughs and rocks everywhere. So from ancient times it has been frequented by tourists seeking their mystery and admiring their scenery. They come to the conclusion that the fantastic pines, the grotesque rocks, the sea of clouds and the hot springs are the four major attractions of the Yellow Mountains. As a matter of fact there are marvels almost everywhere, especially in the following scenic areas: Wenquan (Hot Spring), Yupinglou (Jade Screen Tower), Xihai (West Sea), Beihai (North Sea), Yungusi (Cloud Valley Temple) and Songgu'an (Pine Valley Nunnery).

Owing to the peculiar terrain, the Yellow Mountains's climate is marked by a vertical change, and the vertical distribution of vegetation is also distinctive: plants on the summit, on the middle levels and at the foot belong to the frigid, temperate and subtropical zones respectively. There are more than 1500 species of plants, of which trees comprise one third. So the Yellow Mountains occupy an important place in China's botanical research. Here you will find century-old pines, firs, ginkgoes, Chinese torreyas, Chinese sweet gums, nanmus, camphorwoods and the precious Magua trees, remnants of the glacial era. The Yellow Mountains abound in flowering plants; many of them are rare ones, such as Goddess Flower, the Yellow Mountains Azelea as well as camellia, plum, lily crape myrtle, orchid, Spring Heralding Flower and so on. It has a rich store of medicinal herbs; more than 300 kinds are found here; the notable ones being glossy ganoderma, ginseng, Chinese goldthread rhizome and Chinese cinnamon. Maofeng tea of the Yellow Mountains is well known at home amd abroad.

The Yellow Mountains also provide the natural habitat for a wide variety of fauna. Among the animals there are monkeys, goats, deer and David's deer. There are rare birds such as the red-billed leiothrix, the silver pheasant, the octave-tone bird and the oriole, all good singers. The red-billed leiothrix (called "love birds" in Chinese) are so lovely that they have become favourites of foreign tourists and are exported by pairs. Besides, chukar from the streams is good to make delicious dishes with.

The temperature in Yellow Mountains is agreeable all the year round. It is cool in summer, averaging 20°C at the North Sea Guest-house (1,630 metres above sea) and 25°C at Hot Spring (630 metres above sea) in July (the hottest month). As clouds often shut out the sun, hot weather never stays long, and this makes Yellow Mountains an ideal summer resort.

Though looking fresh and young, Yellow Mountains have a long history to which ancient books, poems and paintings as well as carved inscriptions all bear witness. Li Bai was not the only poet who sang in its praise, Tang poets Jia Dao (779-843) and Du Xunhe (846-907) also came here and wrote poems. In the succeeding dynasties people kept coming and giving expression to their admiration in poetry. Xu Xiake (1586-1641), the great geographer and traveller of the Ming Dynasty, devoted two of his travel notes to Yellow Mountains. Jian Jiang and Shi Tao (1642-1718), master painters of the Xin'an School in the Qing Dynasty, left behind them many paintings. Li Siguang (J.S.Lee 1889-1971), the late celebrated geologist, summed up his personal inspections in his book the Quaternary Glacial Phenomena in Yellow Mountains, Anhui Province". Inscriptions of the past generations meet one's eye here and there: "Clouds in a myriad of forms", "Peaks piercing the sky", "A cool world", "Fantastic and beautiful", "Scenery of exceptional charm", to mention just a few of them. Such poetic phrases in handsome calligraphy are not only decorative, they are themselves part of the fascinating scene.

Today, through government care, Yellow Mountains scenic spots have been renovated and opened to tourists. A longest telpher in the Asia Area at present has been built from the Cloud Valley Temple in the mountains to the White Goose Ridge on the top of the mountains. The mountain paths which used to be dangerous have been repaired and widened, with a total length of more than 50 kilometres. Guesthouses, pavilions and other buildings have sprung up one after another. High-tension lines have been extended to the summit of peaks and a weather station erected on the Brightness Apex.Scientific researches such as geological prospecting, botanical and meteorological survey, medicinal herbs collecting, etc. are carried out by respective work teams from all parts of the country. There are artistic activities here too, with painters, photographers, writers, poets, musicians and actors, Chinese and foreign, coming to do creative work or enrich their experiences.

Beijing

Yellow Mountains

HOT SPRING SCENIC AREA

6. Gate of the Yellow Mountains

Hot Spring of the Yellow Mountains

The Hot Spring of the Yellow Mountains of nationwide fame, was discovered and tapped more than a thousand years ago. Gushing forth from the foot of Purple Cloud Peak, it has never run dry during the most severe droughts nor overflooded during excessive rain. It is of a high-temperature carbonate type, with therapeutic effects for metabolic disorder, cardiovascular disease and malfunctions of digestive, nervous and motorial systems. Its clear waters remain at 42°C all the year round and can be used for drinking and bathing. Baths and swimming pools have been built around the spring.

Thousand Feet Spring . Spring

Heavy rainfalls, steep peaks and sheer cliffs all help to form cataracts, springs, pools and streams in the Yellow Mountains. Baizhangquan (Thousand Feet Spring), Renzipu (Inverted-V Waterfall) and Jiulongpu (Nine Dragons Cataract) are wellknown falls. while Mingxianquan (Ringing String Spring), Sandiequan (Three Folding Spring) and Lingxi Spring excel among the mountain springs. Then there are the famous Qinglongtan (Green Dragon Pool), Bailongtan (White Dragon Pool), Wulongtan (Black Dragon Pool), Laolongtan (Old Dragon Pool), Feicuichi (Jadeite Pool) and Taohuaxi (Peach Blossom Stream). After rain the mountain is particularly alive with gurgling streams, freshets and thunderous falls.

Grotesque Rocks of the Yellow Mountains

On every peak of the Yellow Mountains there are numerous grotesque rock with such vivid names "Immortal Pointing the Way", "Magpie on a Plum Tree", "Eighteen Arhats Facing the South Sea", "Goddess Embroidering", "Immortal Sunning His Boot", "Squirrel Skipping to Celestial Capital", "Golden Cock Crowing towards the Heavenly Gate", "Monkey Gazing at the Sea", "Boy Worshiping Buddha Guanyin" and "Rock Flying from afar", etc, These fantastic rocks turn the Yellow Mountains into a museum of natural sculptures.

These grotesque rocks were created by the nature. Early in the Quaternary Glacier Period, the landforms of the Yellow Mountains underwent great changes. Permeated and eroded by the glacier for millions upon millions of years, some rocks were splited open and others collapsed. Owing to exposure to nature over the years, rocks gradually took various shapes. Huge grotesque rocks with inscriptions such as "Dragon's Head", "Tiger's Head", "Fascination" and "Eternalness" — one sees at Peach Blossom Stream and the lower place of Cloud Valley Temple in the Yellow Mountains — were rushed here by the glacier.

Stone Inscriptions of the Yellow Mountains

Numerous stone inscriptions of past generations are extant. They are specimens of fine calligraphy as well as literary descriptions of the Yellow Mountains scenery: "Clouds in a myriad forms", "Fantastic and beautiful", "Peaks piercing the sky", "A picture painted by the hand of Nature", "Magnificent and fanciful", "Beautiful rivers and mountains", "A roaring stone lion", "Hark! The dragon's roaring", "A recumbent cloud", "Fascinating", "Eternalness", "Intoxicated rock", etc. The last one has a legend behind it: Li Bai, the great Tang poet, was said to be so enraptured by Yellow Mountains scenery that he drank his fill and sang wildly walking around the rock. At last the rock got intoxicated together with the tumbled poet.

Information for Mountain Climbers

As the mountains are high, one should avoid watching scenery while climbing the steep paths. Stop to enjoy the scenery before resuming the climb. It is advisable to wear sneakers or cloth shoes. Leather-sole shoes, slippers or plastic-sole shoes are unsuitable for climbing.

Do not open your umbrella at wind gap when you climb the mountains and stop climbing in a thunderstrom.

Do not litter so as to keep the mountains clean.

It is advisable to carry walking stick, flask, some food and raincoat or umbrella on a climbing trip.

Cotton-padded coats can be leased at the tourist service centres to keep warm against the cold in the morning and evening on the peaks. Walking sticks can be bought at shops at Tangkou and Hot Spring.

JADE SCREEN TOWER
SCENIC AREA

22. Three Islets of Fairyland

24. Jade Screen Peak in the First
    Sunlight

25. Jade Screen Peak in Spring
26. Jade Screen Peak in Autumn

Average Monthly Temperatures on the Yellow Mountains

As the Yellow Mountains scenery changes with the alternation of the four seasons, tourists can choose any time to come to the Yellow Mountains and find the best sights of the season to enjoy.

Month Average Temperatures
at 1800 Metres above Sea Level

January	-3.2°C
February	-1.8°C
March	4.7°C
April	7.9°C
May	11.7°C
June	14.8°C
July	17.7°C
August	17.3°C
September	13.7°C
October	8.9°C
November	3.9°C
December	-0.7°C

N.B. From 1,800 metres, every 100 metres down in altitude registers a 0.7°C rise on the thermometer.

28. On the Crucian Carp's Back
29. Buddhist Halo over the Jade Screen Peak

30. Distant View of the East Sea from the Peak of Celestial Capital
31. Heavenly Pond

HEAVENLY SEA SCENIC AREA

32. Magnificent View of the Heavenly
    Sea

36. Jade Islet in the Heaven

37. Distant View of the Clouds Gate Peak

38. Distant View of the Peak of Celestial Capital

WHITE CLOUD STREAM SCENIC AREA

39 West Sea Gully

40. Human World in the Heaven
41. Treasures Deposited on the Bottom
   of the Sea

WEST SEA SCENIC AREA

42. Wandering among the Peaks

Names of the 72 Peaks of the Yellow Mountains

1. Alchemy Peak
2. Celestial Capital Peak
3. Green Phoenix Peak
4. Alms Bowl Peak
5. Purple Stone Peak
6. Purple Cloud Peak
7. Clear Pool Peak
8. Peach Blossom Peak
9. Cloud Gate Peak
10. Floating Mound Peak
11. Cloud Edge Peak
12. Holy Spring Peak
13. Cinnabar Peak
14. Lotus Peak
15. Rongcheng Peak
16. Stone Figure Peak
17. Stone Pillar Peak
18. Pine Forest Peak
19. Stone Bed Peak
20. Beyond Clouds Peak
21. Rosy Cloud Peak
22. Stone Gate Peak
23. Chess Piece Peak
24. Lion Peak
25. Immortal Peak
26. Ascending Peak
27. Fairy Capital Peak
28. Xuanyuan Peak
29. Immortal Watching Peak
30. Bushui Peak
31. Rows of Mountains Peak
32. Green Peak
33. Nine Dragons Peak
34. Lotus Peak
35. Flying Dragon Peak
36. Quarrying Peak
37. Huge Turtle Peak
38. Lotus Pistil Peak
39. Ox Nose Peak
40. Jade Screen Peak
41. Ploughing Cloud Peak
42. Old Man Peak
43. Toad Peak
44. Eyebrow Peak
45. Buddha's Palm Peak
46. Incense Burner Peak
47. Frog Peak
48. Folded-Palms Peak
49. White Goose Peak
50. Stalagmite Peak
51. Beginning-to-Believe Peak
52. Thin Sword Peak
53. Camel Back Peak
54. Guanyin Peak
55. Cock Peak
56. Bookcase Peak
57. Pagoda Peak
58. Sedan-Chair Roof Peak
59. Five Old Men Peak
60. Window Peak
61. Scholar Peak
62. Recumbent Cloud Peak
63. Pillow Peak
64. First Class Peak
65. Taoist Priest Peak
66. Drunken Man Peak
67. Needle Peak
68. Millstone Peak
69. Arhat Peak
70. Writing Brush Peak
71. Leaning Peak
72. Stone Drum Peak

45. Buddhist Halo over the West Sea
46. Cliffs and Deep Valley

47. Fantastic Peak in the Sunset Glow

48. Immortal Sunning His Boot
49. Peaks at the West Sea

50. Scissors Peak

52. Jade Tower in the Fairy Mountain

53. West Sea in the Sunset Glow
54. Cloud-Dispelling Pavilion

Sea of Clouds of the Yellow Mountains

As the Yellow Mountains Range is high and dense with lush forests and has plenty of rainfall, it can be seen wrapped in misty clouds in all four seasons of the year, for about two thirds of the time. Therefore, the Yellow Mountains are also called "yun Hai" (Sea of Clouds) which is geographically divided into North Sea, West Sea, East Sea, Heavenly Sea and Front Sea. These seas of clouds, vast and misty, billowing and surging, veil the valleys and mountains and allow only the peaks to show like green islands over their boundless foamy expanses. At daybreak, the rising sun casts its golden rays on the silver sea of clouds, making the Yellow Mountains Range even more enchanting.

56. North Sea

57. Cool World

58. Cool Terrace
59. Ascending Peak
60. A Flower Growing out of a Writing
    Brush in Dream

61. Clouds Roaming in the Yellow Mountains
62. Waterfall Clouds
63. Distant View of the North Sea Guest-house

65. Clearing up after Snowing
66. Bookcase Peak

67. Monkey Gazing at the Sea

68. North Sea in Winter
69. Pines and Mountains Covered by Ice
    and Snow

70. North Sea in Autumn
71. Yellow Mountains after Rain

SHIXIN PEAK SCENIC AREA

72. Recumbent Dragon Pine in Winter

73. Magnificent Scenery
74. Fantastic Mountains

75. Harp Pine
76. Rime

The Yellow Mountains' Rime

Snow-falls on the Yellow Mountains concentrate in January and February. But snow can hardly stay on trees, for it is soon swept away by strong winds. When the wind drops, however, mist rises and freezes into frost which thickly coasts the pines. the Yellow Mountains rime scenes are really a marvel. You seem to be in a crystal world, and your eyes are dazzled by the glittering light all round.

77. Recumbent Dragon Pine
78. Immortals Having a Game of Chess

Pines of The Yellow Mountains

The pine of the Yellow Mountains is a variety of Chinese pine created by the special environment of the mountain.

It is said that on every rock there is a pine and that every pine has its peculiar form. Pines grown on high altitudes from 800 metres above sea level upwards, most of them at 1,500 — 1,7500 metres on northern slopes and at 1,000 — 1,600 metres on southern slopes.

The most notable Yellow Mountains pines are: Yingkesong (Greeting Pine in front of Lion Stone at Jade Screen Tower), Songkesong (Farewell Pine to the right of Jade Screen Tower), Putuansong (Hassock Pine in Lotus Gully), Feng-huangsong (Phoenix Pine in Heavenly Sea), Qipansong (Chessboard Pine at Pingtian Stone Bridge), Jieyinsong (Usher Pine on Beginning-to-Believe Peak), Qilinsong (Unicorn Pine, on the way from North Sea Guesthouse to Cool Terrace), Heihusong (Black Tiger Pine, on the way from North Sea Guesthouse to Beginning-to-Believe Peak), Tanhaisong or Wusong (Probe-the-Sea or Dancer Pine by Crucian Carp's Back on Celestial Capital and Wolongsong(RecumbentDragon Pine below Beginning-to-Believe Peak). These are the ten most famous pines of Yellow Mountains. Of course, they are only representatives, for you can count famous pines by the thousand, each with its own distinct beauty and grace.

The fantastic forms of Yellow Mountains pines have a lot to do with the natural environment. The rugged terrain with a host of cliffs and crags makes it very difficult for pines to grow straight, so they have to twist, bend or sometimes even stretch downwards.

In order to resist strong winds and withstand frost and ice, they usually grow a flat top with short, hardy needles forming a dark green mass, and their trunks and boughs are both tough and resilient. There is another peculiarity: swept by the wind, or attacted by the sun, many pines branch out only on one side.

These graceful but sturdy pines have to fight very hard for their existence. There being little soil on the peaks, they have to strike roots deep into crevices to draw water and nourishment. The roots are often several times the length of the trunk. And they are able to absorb nitrogen, phosphorus and potassium from granite. With such deep roots, they stand firm on the rocks, braving wind and snow and remaining evergreen.

81. Pine with Joining Branches
82. Pine with Hanging Branches

Seeing off Hermit Wen
Back to Former Residence
White Goose Peak
in the Yellow Mountains

by Li Bai (701-762)

Thousands of feet high towers the Yellow Mountains
With its thirty-two magnificent peaks,
Blooming like golden lotus flowers
Amidst red crags and rock columns.
Once I was on its lofty summit,
Admiring Tianmu Pine below.
The place is still traceable where the immortal
Before ascending to heaven made elixir out of jade.
Now you embark on your journey there alone—
Another Wen Boxue* I happened to meet—
Who've been to Five Mountains for beauty of nature,
Leaving behind countless ranges of hills.
Homeward you go—back to White Goose Ridge,
Back to drink from your Elixir Well.
If by chance I pay you a visit,
I expect to be met by your light carriage.
Eastwards from Lingyang you bend your steps,
And pick your way through fragrant bushes,
Many a stream and many a ford,
Peaks upon peaks shutting out the sky—
That's where I'll call on you some other day
Across a bridge that spans cliffs like a rainbow.
   *Wen Boxue, mentioned by Zhuang Zi as a
wise scholar contemporary with Confucius.

84. Cloud Sea and Pine Waves

85. Peaks Encircled by the Floating
    Clouds

CLOUD VALLEY TEMPLE SCENIC AREA

86. Back Mountains in Early Autumn

Telpher from the Cloud Valley Temple to White Goose Ridge

From the Cloud Valley Temple (890m. above sea level) in the Yellow Mountains to the White Goose Ridge at the east end of North Sea there runs a passenger telpher with a hypotenuse of 2803.96m. and a difference of 772.80m. between the two termini up and low. It is the longest running cable car in Asia. The cable car carries 40 persons at a time. One way trip takes eight minutes while it takes one four hours to reach from the cloud Valley Temple to the White Goose Ridge on foot.

There are ten huge characters caved on the Standing Horse Peak (also called Green Phoenix Peak) which means: on the Standing Horse Peak, one commands a distant view of the East Sea and overlooks the nearby Taiping County. No visitor leaves unimpressed by the awe-inspiring huge stone inscription.

88. Autumn Scene
89. Magpie on a Plum Tree

Flowers in the Yellow Mountains

Since the climate changes vertically in the Yellow Mountains, the flowers here take turns blossoming during all the four seasons. Goddess Flower is rarely seen elsewhere and Yellow Mountains' Azelea is famous in China. Camellia is white and red, Spring Heralding Flower has silver petals with purple brim and Mountain Yinghua Flower is cerise. There are also Greem Plum, Small Orchid, Lily and Winter Jasmine growing in the Yellow Mountains. Even in winter when the mountains are covered with snow, Mountain Wintersweets still blossom at the North Sea 1600m. above sea level, which is trully a sight of wonder.

91. Goddess Flower
92. Spring Heralding Flower.
93. Orchid
94. Azelea

95. Phoenix-tail Butterflies
96. Octave-tone Birds

Love Birds

The Yellow Mountains lie on an important route of migrating birds. In early spring or late autumn large groups of red – billed leiothrix comming from afar like to make a stop – over here. These rare love birds pair off wing to wing and sing joyously. If left alone a single bird looks lovesick and won't sing any more. Some are exported abroad by pairs. Other rare birds include the silver pheasant and the Bayinniao (the octave-tone bird) which are generally known as the Yellow Mountains musician.

97. Love Birds

99. A Monk
100. Photographers
101. Night on the Eve of the Spring
Festival

A Travel Guide of the Yellow Mountains

The Yellow Mountains is noted for its infinite enchanting scenery and particularly its peaks of fantastic shapes. Here, the scenery varies from season to season and as the peaks grow and fall. Unlike other scenic areas where the view is all in sight, the Yellow Mountains offers a constant changing panorama that stirs up vivid imagination. This guide will come in handy for all those who are interested in exploring the beauty of the Yellow Mountains.

Upon entering the mountain flower-flanked Gate of the Yellow Mountains after driving through Tangkou of Shexian County in southern Anhui, one comes to the scenic area, and then to the Hot Spring which lies a little distance ahead.

Six hundred and thirty meters above the sea level, the Hot Spring has a large tourist complex, including the Yellow Mountains Guesthouse, Taoyuan Guesthouse, Xuanyuan Hotel, the Hot Spring Bath, the Hot Spring Swimming Pool, the Postal-telecommunications Building, villas and tourist shops. The scenic area straddles the Peach Blossom Brook that flows between Purple Cloud Peak and Peach Blossom Peak. Across the brook are the Purple Cloud Bridge, the Scenery Watching Bridge, the Famous Spring Bridge and the White Dragon Bridge. Scattered around are the Fish Watching Pavilion, Falls Watching Pavilion, Peach Blossom Land Pavilion, and the Falls Watching Tower. Here one can watch Thousand Feet Spring and Inverted V Falls as well as Celestial Capital Peak, Lotus Peak, Cinnabar Peak, Purple Cloud Peak and Purple Rock Peak. Going up along the brook, one will see such scenic spots as Roaring Lion Rock, Dragon Head Rock, Tiger Head Rock, the Red Well, Intoxicated Rock, Sword Testing Rock as well as Green Dragon Pool, White Dragon Pool, Three Folding Spring and Ringing String Spring.

Departing from the Hot Spring, travelers can take two routes for mountain sightseeing: One is to ascend the imposing and steep mountain front and then descend the picturesque back mountains and then return to the Hot Spring. The other is just to take the opposite route.

Let's now take the first route. Passing the stone tablet engraved with the characters of "Beautiful Rivers and Mountains", which is to the right of Yiran Pavilion, one reaches the ancient Mercy Light Temple after crossing the serene bamboo grove and the Dragon Turning Back Bridge. To the left of the Temple stands Toad Peak, and behind the Temple, the Cinnabar Peak. Nearby, there is the Draping Cloud Bridge, Fayan Spring and the Thousand Monk Stove. A statue of Xu Xiake, the great traveler and geographer of the Ming Dynasty,

stands in the temple in commemoration of his two trips to the Yellow Mountains ih 1616 and 1618.

Farther way up is the Golden Sand Hill. At the foot of the hill one can see Yinggu Rock. To the left of the road is the Cave Flying From Afar and to the right is Candle Peak. Crossing the ceve and then the Crescent Pavilion, one finds the Head Knocking Rock. Above the rock in the right direction, one can see traces of the mountain movement of the glacial period half way at Green Phoenix Peak. Further along the road is the Green Phoenix Bridge. Standing on the bridge, one can look up and see the Crucian Carp Back, which is the most perilous point of the Celestial Capital Peak. Turning back, one sees below the Water Screen Cave on Peach Blossom Peak. Crossing the bridge and going through the Drum Beating Cave leads one to the Half Way Up the Mountain Temple.

The temple is located between Old Man Peak and Cinnabar Peak at 1,340 meters above the sea level. One can take a rest and have some tea here before resuming the tour. Looking up in front of the temple, one sees a rock resembling a flying and crowing cock on the Celestial Capital Peak and facing the Heavenly Threshold. This is just the famous grotesque rock "Golden Cock Crowing towards the Heavenly Gate" one can also see the stone engraving of "Hearing a Cock Crowing in the Sky" on the rock. Leaving the Half Way Up the Mountain Temple, one may take the new route leading to the Celestial Capital Peak (The old route is to go to the Dragon Slope, pass the Heavenly Threshold , cross the Cloud Nest Cave and then reach the foot of Celestial Capital Peak and climb to the apex of the Celestial Capial Peak.). First one comes to the Tiger Mouth (also known as Guts Testing Wall), and steps on the narrow Three Folding Path. Here, one can see a rock resembling two monks worshiping the Buddha. One may proceed to cross the Three Ladies Cave and climb up the rocky path where the sky seems within reach, to be greeted by an ancient pine. A narrow pines flanked path leads one to the Bell Tower where the rocks ring with bell sounds. After crossing the Springboard Rock, one finally ascends the Celestial Capital Peak, one of the three main peaks of the Yellow Mountains. The Celestial Capital Peak rises 1,829 meters high, piercing the clouds. Hence the name. It is ideal for taking a bird-eye view of the unfolding magnificent landscape of the Yellow Mountains. Therefore, one can not claim to have been to the Yellow Mountains without reaching the Celestial Capital Peak.

Descending the Celestial Capital Peak westwards, travelers go through the Immortal Gate Keeper Cave with vivid peach resembling rock formation on the cave, pass Crucian Carp Peak formed during the glacial period and cross the Heavenly Bridge where the Sea Exploring Pine stands. Further down, visitors come to the Heavenly Jade Screen. A half-kilometer long Heavenly Stairs consisting of stairs, stone railings and iron chains winds down the cliff. At the Bottom of the stairs one sees a scene of kid Worshiping the Buddha Guanyin and then reaches the foot of the Celestial Capital Peak.

Turning left from the foot of the Celestial Capital Peak, one steps onto the Jade Screen Stairs and goes through the Care Slope, passes Hassock Rock, crosses the Lying Cloud Cave and the Immortal Bridge before reaching a place called A Thread of Sky. As the path here is caught between cliffs, it is so narrow as to allow passage of only one person. Looking above, the sky is reduced to a barely seen thread, hence the name. When one looks back upon leaving the path, three exquisite rocks with several lovely young pines embraced by fleeting clouds come into sight. This fairy scene is refered to as the Three Islets of Fairyland. After crossing Manjusri Cave, one sees the famous Greeting Pine and the Jade Screen Tower.

The Jade Screen Tower stands against the 1,668 meter high Jade Screen Peak. Originally the seat of Manjusri Temple, it is now a tourist center with complete service facilities. Around the Tower are elephant and lion shaped rocks and ancient pines. In front of the Tower there emerge to the left the Celestial Capital Peak and Ploughing Cloud Peak. On Ploughing Cloud Peak there is a rock which looks likes a squirrel jumping at the Celestial Capital Peak. Below the peak there is another odd shaped rock which conjures up a scene of an immortal getting off a sedan chair. To the right are Lotus Peak, Lotus Pistil Peak and Holy Spring Peak. Viewed from distance, the rock on Lotus Pistil Peak looks like a small boating sailing through the ocean of clouds. Beside the peak there stands a rock that resembles a peacock playing in the lotus. Standing on the terrace in front of the pine, one is greeted by a panorama of numerous peaks and rocks half hidden in the clouds. Therefore, a visit to the Jade Screen Tower has long been considered a must for a tour of the Yellow Mountains.

The Jade Screen Tower is a half way stop between the Hot Spring and the West Sea and North Sea scenic areas. Going further ahead, tourists pass the Farewell Pine and the Hassock Pine. If one looks back, an ox shaped rock on Ox Nose Peak comes into sight. The scene is knowe as Rhinocerros Watching the Moon. The distance from Jade Screen Peak down to the bottom of the Lotus Ravine is about two and half kilometers. Here the terrain rises. Climbing up

several hundred steps stairs, one reaches Lotus Ridge. Standing above in the right direction is Lotus Peak.

With a height of 1,873 meters, lotus Peak is the highest peak of the Yellow Mountains. It is embradeɖ by small hills, resembling the lotus, hence the name. A one and half kilometer long winding path links Lotus Ridge and the apex of lotus Peak. One needs to cross four caves on the way up before reaching the apex. Pines in the shape of flying dragons and double dragons as well as the Yellow Mountain Azalea are found on the peak. Standing together in the central part of the Yellow Mountains, the magnificent lotus Peak, Brightness Apex and the Celestial Capital Peak unfold in all their majesty.

Going down the same route northwards, one passes turtle shaped and snake shaped rocks and reaches the One Hundred Step Cloud Stairs. Here, a scene of a rock resembling an old monk watching the sea under the opposite Rongcheng Peak is seen. Getting off the stairs and crossing the Lotus Cave and Huge Turtle Cave, one comes to the Heavenly Sea. To the left of the site of Central Sea Pavilion stands Stone Column Peak, and to the right is the Phoenix Pine. Going up for a while along the stone stairway, one can then look back at the famous rock sight known as Huge Turtle Carrying a Golden Turtle on Its Back. Further up in the right direction there stands Alchemy Peak and the 1,840.9 meter high Brightness Apex, the second tallest peak of the Yellow Mountains. With Brightness Apex towering above the clouds, one commands a majestic view of a sea of ridges, peaks and gullies below.

Taking the west route or north route from Brightness Apex, visitors may tour the West Sea or North Sea, two famous scenic areas of the Yellow Mountains, and stay at the West Sea Hotel or North Sea Guesthouse. The following is what visitors can see on the west route:

Descending Brightness Apex, one comes to the West Sea via a newly opened tourist route. A mystical Peak Flying From Afar first comes into sight, with a huge 10 meter high rock weighing 600 tons standing on it. Passing several peaks nearby, visitors arrive at the Dispelling Cloud Pavilion where one commands an excellent view of the unfolding scene. There stand in front of the pavilion a sea of variously shaped peaks that inspire all sorts of fairy imagination. These architectural wonders of the nature turn the whole West Sea into a natural art gallery. When the sun sets, the whole valley basks in a myriad of sun rays, becoming a famous scene of the Yellow Mountains. Equally impressive is the 1,712 meter high Rosy Clouds Peak behind the Dispelling Cloud Pavilion. Standing on the peak, one can watch the sun rising above the cloud and Peak Flying From

Afar and Nine Dragon Peak in all their grandeur.

The West Sea, long known as the Mystery Valley for the many clusters of peaks and the fathomless depth of the valley, has been opend up as the White Cloud Stream Scenic Area.The seven kilometer long newly paved staircase extends from the Hook Bridge Nunnery inside the West Gate of the Yellow Mountains, across the bottom of the valley, and reaches the newly built Central Sea Pavilion at the Heavenly Sea. Tourists may go to Qianxun Falls via the Hook Bridge Nunnery and the Shy Spring. The highest falls in the Yellow Mountains, Qianxun Falls have a drop of 140 meters, and is ice free all the year round. The falls thunder can be heard at Swan Rock near the brook and one can also have a near look on the "Immortal Walking on Stilts". Passing the Dropping Spring and the Lucky Cloud Bridge, one comes to the Dispelling Cloud Pavilion. Then, a twisting path leads one through Buxian Bridge and to the Goddess Flower Bed and finally to the Central Sea Pavilion at the Heavenly Sea. On the way, one can watch pines in all kinds of odd shapes.

The North Sea is just a few kilometers away from the Dispelling Cloud Pavilion in the West Sea, with the Yellow Mountains West Sea Hotel on the way. The North Sea Guesthouse is located near Lion Peak, at an altitude of 1,630 meters above sea level.

In the Dawn Pavilion in front of the guesthouse, one may enjoy the beautiful scenery of Beginning to Believe Peak and Goddess Peak as well as the Stalagmite Bridge that inspire imagination of various fairy scenes. To the right of the guesthouse is the Flower House. In front of it is the Sunken Flower Bed with many rocks of fantastic shapes in it. Turning left from the guesthouse and passing the Unicorn Pine leads one onto the Cooling Terrace and Lion Peak. Reaching out from the cliff and facing the valley in three directions, the terrace is an ideal place for watching sunrise and the sea of clouds. Atop the Cooling Apex of Lion Peak, one can look down at the rocks on Pingding Hill which is famous for resembling a scene of a monkey watching the sea. Below Lion Peak is the Ten Thousand Pines Forest which sends out constant pine soughing. Turing right from the guesthouse, while viewing various ancient pines on the way, one crosses the Immortal Bridge and ascends Beginning to Believe Peak. Here, a magnificent view of stalagmites unfold itself.

Leaving the North Sea Guesthouse and descending the mountain path right of the Cooling Terrace, visitors may proceed to the Pine Valley Nunnery Scenic Area at the bottom of the North Sea. Following the winding Eighteen Fold Path and crossing the Flower Brook and Bird Valley, one sees the swan and brush shaped rocks, and then Camel Peak on the left. At the Three Way Pavilion, one may view the three Buddha shaped rocks on Pagoda Peak to the east. Further ahead, there are peaks on the left resembling cock, bookcase, medicine case and sedan chair roof. To the right of the Two Way Pavilion, there are two scenes known as "the Immortals Watching the Poster" and "the Poet Li Bai Gets Drunk". The Pine Valley Nunnery lies ahead of the One Way Pavilion. On the way to Lotus Ridge two and half kilometers away, one sees a number of pools, such as the Jadeite Pool, the Black Dragon Pool, the White Dragon Pool and the Aged Dragon Pool along the brook. The water scene is most enchanting at the Jadeite Pool, which, it is said, used to be the bathing place of the ocean dragon princess.

To go to the Cloud Valley Temple Scenic Area in the East Sea, one needs to turn left from the North Sea Guesthouse and go eastwards. Passing the Black Tiger Pine, visitors reach White Goose Ridge, and the beautiful and steep White Goose Peak stands in the left direction. White Goose Ridge is the terminal of the newly installed 2803.96 meter long cable car route between the Cloud Valley Temple and the North Sea. Traveling on the telpher gives one a bird-eye view of the East Sea. Those who prefer to walk may down the valley and appreciate the scenery on the way. Descending White Goose Ridge, one is greeted by numerous rocks of bizarre shapes around the brook as well as picturesque valley scene consisting of woods and springs. Passing the Fascination Pavilion, the Cloud Valley Temple is in sight.

Situated between Arhat Peak and Incense Burner Peak, the 890 meter high Cloud Valley Temple is a half way stop in the back mountains on the way back from the North Sea to the Hot Spring as well as the departure station of the cable car route to the North Sea. Tourists going both ways may stay at the hotels here. In particular, the Cloud Valley Mountain Villa, a newly built spacious building in the traditional local architectural style of the Ming Dynasty, provides comfortable service for tourists. Here, one can also see the rare aged yellow Chinese fir and iron Chinese fir and enjoy the Yellow Mountains Maofeng, a famous local tea. Descending the mountain path to the left of the Cloud Valley Temple and going through the bamboo grove, tourists can watch the Nine Dragon Falls four kilometers away.

On the way back from the Cloud Valley Temple, one can stop to watch the pouring and thunderous Thousead Feet Falls at close distance before finally returning to the Hot Spring.

A Sketch Tour Map of the Yellow Mountains

Distances Between Different Scenic Spots in the Yellow Mountains

Gate of Yellow Mountains — Hot Spring	3 li
Hot Spring — Ciguang Tower	3 li
Ciguang Tower — Banshan Temple	5 li
Banshan Temple — Top of Tiandu Peak	2.2 li
Top of Tiandu Peak — Foot of Tiandu Peak	13 li
Foot of Tiandu Peak — Jade Screen Tower	2 li
Jade Screen Tower — Foot of Lotus Peak	5 li
Foot of Lotus Peak — Top of Lotus Peak — Heavenly Sea	5 li
Heavenly Sea — North Sea Guest House	5 li
North Sea Guest House — West Sea	3 li
Diaoqiao Nunnery — Haixin Pavilion	14 li
Haixin Pavilion — Peak Flying from Afar — Paiyun Pavilion	5 li
North Sea Guest House — Pine Valley Nunnery	20 li
North Sea Guest House — Cloud Valley Temple	15 li
Cloud Valley Temple — Nine Dragone Fall	8 li
Cloud Valley Temple — Hot Spring	15 li

91

A Survey of Scenic Areas of Huangshan City

Huangshan (the Yellow Mountains) City borders on Zhejiang and Jiangxi Provinces. It has under its jurisdiction three districts (Tunxi, Huangshan and Huizhou) and four counties (Shexian, Yixian, Xiuning and Qimen), which cover much of the area used to be known as Huizhou. The Yellow Mountains also reach some areas in Taiping and other nearby counties.

The scenery of the Yellow Mountains unfolds as they extend. Flowing in front of the Mountains is the blue Xin'an River. In the back there lies the placid Taiping Lake. At the eastern end of the Mountains is situated the Qingliang Peak Nature Reserve. The Guniujiang Nature Reserve is located at the western end of the Mountains. On both sides of the southern slopes are the quiet and secluded Yixian County and Shexian County known for their historical and cultural heritage. Further ahead, right to the south is the river town of Tunxi District, which is the seat of the Huangshan Municipal Government. To the southwest lies Qiyun Mountain which to be known as Baiyue.

These picturesque scenic areas are crisscrossed with roads, railways and winding brooks and dotted with aged houses, streets, bridges, stone stelae, pagodas, temples and birthplaces of historical figures. The region is also easily accessible by air.

Huangshan is renowned as the natural world park and a history museum. The following are sketches of the scenic spots.

Houses of the Ming and Qing Dynasties (16th-19th Century) in Yixian County. As it is hidden in the mountain, Yixian County is known as a land of peach blossoms, meaning a haven of peace in Chinese literature. On entering the county, one hardly spots any houses along the stream between the green hills. However, going through the hill passes, open base land comes into sight where over 3,000 well-preserved pre-20th Century houses stand. These clusters of aged houses are acclaimed by tourists and scholars as the most beautiful villages in the world and a treasure house of the traditional Chinese housing structure.

Xidi Village and Hong Village attract particular attention for their famed houses.

The layout of Xidi Village is well planed. There are in the village 122 houses in black, white and gray colors built in the 18th and 19th Centuries. Each has whitewashed walls, both low and high, elaborated-shaped eaves and courtyard within courtyard. The gate, halls and windows display typical features of local wood, brick and stone carving. Of particular interest is a gilded balcony overreaching into the lane at Dafudi. It was said that anyone fortunate enough to pick up the colorful ball thrown by the young lady from the balcony could win her love. With all the back lanes, houses and ditches connecting with one another, it takes a while for a visitor to find one's way around. Standing tall at the village entrance is the Hu Wenguang Stone Archway. A single-structured and four storied building that is divided into three parts and supported by four pillars, the archway is a masterpiece of the Ming Dynasty architecture, testifying to the past prosperity of the village.

Not far from Xidi Village is Hong Village which is also famed for its pre-20th Century buildings. What is unique about the village is that it is ox-shaped. The high ground is like an ox head, the ancient trees like ox horns and bridges like ox hoofs. The houses form the body, and the river is like an ox tail. The 1,000 meter long zigzagging water channel is compared to ox intestine, and the Moon Pool and the scenic Nanhu Lake take the shape of ox stomach. Thanks to the plentiful supply of water, flowers and fruits are grown in abundance in courtyards, with water corridors winding through them. Fish is also raised in the pond.

In addition, the pre-20th Century houses in Xi Wu, ancestral halls in Nanping and Pingshan, bamboo grove in Mukeng as well as the birthplaces of many historical figures and contemporary celebrities are also popular toursit spots.

Town of historical and cultural renown in Shexian County. Shexian County was set up back in the Qin Dynasty over 2,000 years ago, which was the seat of the local government in the Tang, Song, Yuan Ming and Qing Dynasties. In those days it was also popularly known as Huizhou. Throughout history, it is the political, economic and cultural center of the southern mountain region of Anhui Province. The growth of local commerce reached its peak during the Ming and Qing Dynasties, and the town became famous nationwide for its wealth. Because of its rich historical and cultural heritage as well as the numerous scenic spots, the Chinese Government designated Shexian County as one of the cities and towns of historical and cultural renown in China.

Two pagodas of the Song Dynasty. Changqing Temple Pagoda stands high at the foot of Xigan Hill along the Lianjiang River. Filled with earth inside, it is an imposing square-shaped seven storied pagoda, with color Buddhist images painted on the wall and elaborate eaves at the pagoda top. The iron decorations hanging on the eaves sound like bell in the gentle wind. Xinzhou Pagoda is a simple and smooth designed stone structure in the western part of the town. There are diamond shaped stone eaves on each of the five stories and Buddhist inscriptions on the pagoda surface. Both pagodas are over 800 years old.

Three age-old bridges. They are Taiping Bridge, Wannian Bridge and Ziyang Bridge. These stone arch bridges built in the Ming Dynasty stand across the LianjiangRiver that flowsaround the town. With a length of 279.87 meters, Taiping Bridge has two lanes and 16 arches.

Three wonders of the traditional architecture. They refer to stone archways, ancestral halls and age-old houses.

Built in the Ming Dynasty, Xuguo Stone Archway located in the county town is under government preservation because of its cultural importance. It is a well-designed big four directional stone archway supported by eight pillars, with all the beams linking one another. The three storied front archway and back archway are each supported by two pillars, and the three storied side archways are each supported by two pillars. Exquisite patterns of rare animals and birds are carved on the archway. Leaning ageinst the pillars are 12 vividly carved stone lions.

There stand seven archways (two of the Ming Dynasty and five of the Qing Dynasty) on the road in Tangyue Village in the western suburb. Also in TangyueVillage there are two ancestral halls, one for the male ancestors and other for female ancestors. And it is rare to find an ancestral hall for female ancestors only. Located on the gorgeous Purple Clouds Peak, Qiankou (now changed as Huizhou

District) boasts of age-old houses and ancestral halls. The rugged looking houses stand in interesting contrast with the supporting poles which have delicate flower patterns carved on them. All the visiting scholars, both Chinese and foreign, consider this to be an important place to study the traditional Chinese architecture.

Traditional Chinese architectural structures such as pavilions, towers, and gardens are found everywhere in Shexian County, such as the famous Octagonal Pavilion, Raolu Pavilion, Taibai Pavilion, Tangan Garden, just to name a few.Scenic spots like Wuliao Hill, Xigan Hill,Wenzheng Hill, Qingliang Peak, the Xin'an River, Fengle Lake are all popular tourist spots. This land of cultural heritage has produced many famous artists and personalities of distinction, such as Jian Jiang, founder of the Xin'an School of traditional Chinese painting, his successors Huang Binhong and Wang Caibai and the great Chinese educator Tao Xingzhi. Naturally, one mustn't forget the renowned four treasures of the study (writing brush, ink stick, ink slab and paper) made in Shexian County.

The hill town of Tunxi. Tunxi is the seat of the Huangshan Municipal Government. The lush Huashan Hill and Yangmei Hill lie across the city. The Xin'an River which is joined by Hengjiang River and Lu River flows through the city. Hence, Tunxi is also known as a river town. It is today a garden city as well as the tourist center of Southern Anhui. Tunxi has been a strategic location throughout the past dynasties. It became a thriving commercial city in the Ming and Qing Dynasties when trade was most prosperous in Anhui. The old street which is also referred to as Song Town in an epitome of its glorious past. The old street is stone slab paved and about 1,000 meters long. On both sides of the street are shops in classical Ming and Qing architectural style, with resplendent halls, exquisite pavilions, carved doors and windows, black tiles and whitewashed walls. This plus the Xin'an River nearby provides the living history of the social life of the Ming and Qing Dynasties as well as ideal background for shooting films of classical themes. Over 20 films and TV plays based on classical Chinese works have been shot here. Tunxi is also the birthplace of many renowned historical figures. There is here the residence of Cheng Dawei, a famous Ming mathematician as well as the magnificent residence of Cheng Minzheng, a noted Ming writer. The memorial museum for Dai zhen, a famous Qing philosopher, is also in Tunxi. These places are frequented by visitors. What is also worth mentioning is that the factory making the famous Anhui ink stick is also located in Tunxi. The factory has over 7,800 mould plates for making ink stick, which are considered national treasure.

Qiyun Mountain Covering an area of about 60 kilometers, Qiyun Mountain is located to the west of the county town of Xiuning. The mountain, known as Baiyue in ancient times, is noted for the Taoist activities associated with it over the last 1,000 years. There are 36 gorgeous peaks, 72 bizarre shaped rocks and a beautiful Cloud Rock Lake on the mountain, offering a panorama of the best of hilly scenery. The famous rock calligraphy carving on the mountain has attracted numerous literary figures over the centuries. Li Bai, Zhu Xi, Xu Xiake, and other famous literary figures all wrote poems or proses in praise of the mountain. While only 585 meters above sea level, It has unique attraction because of its Taoist association. The pilgrims will have to pass through three pavilions and three heavenly gates on the ascent before reaching the top. Thus, the excitement of getting closer to the Taoist God is aroused. Many scenic spots and buildings on the mountain have Taoist names, such as God Watching Pavilion, the Cave of Eight Immortals, the Immortal Bridge, the Heavenly Palace, Incense Burner Peak, Drum Peak, etc. They all add to the mystic touch of the scenery.

Qiyun Mountain is also well known for its 700-odd pieces of stone calligraphy carvings of various styles that are found in the halls and peaks . On the stone archway at Arhat Cave there are well-preserved inscriptions carved over 800 years ago. On the Qiyun Rock there are two huge characters of "Cloud Rock" which were carved over 750 years ago in the Song Dynasty. One also sees in front of the Yuxu Palace a stone tablet with inscriptions of 960 characters in it. The prose was written by Tang Yin, a bright young writer in the Ming Dynasty, and it took two years to carve it on the stone tablet. The stone tablet is the biggest of its kind in the south.

The Xin'an River. The eastwards blue line one sees on the tourist map of Huangshan City indicates the Xin'an River. It originates from Liugujian Peak which is 1363 meters above sea level in Huaiyu Mountain of Xiuning County. The brook expands as it rolls down, joining the Hengjiang River at Tunxi. Here, it becomes the 200 kilometer long gently flowing Xin'an River. Sailing on the river, one sees houses of Anhui style with white wall and black tiles here and there on both sides. The fir, bamboo, tea tree, tung tree, loquat and orange forests on the hills extend as far as eye can see, displaying a charming landscape.

The Xin'an River is a major waterway of vital importance to the local economy, shipping out timber and local agricultural produce and transporting in salt and manufactured goods. Tunxi, Yuliang Town and Shendu in Shexian County along the river used to be bustling river ports in the old days. There is still in Yuliang Town a one kilometer long Old Street which used to be the marketplace.

There are numerous scenic spots along the Xin'an River. At Bingtan which is close to the river source, there is the mausoleum of Wang Youdun, an imperial minister in the Qing Dynasty who was a native of Xiuning. Standing around the mausoleum are carved stone human figures, horses, tigers, sheep and lions with graphic features. In Tunxi and Shexian County, the river embraces ancient pavilions and bridges as well as clusters of lakes. Further down the river, one sees both busy rural and urban scenes. On the lower reaches of the Xin'an River there is the pearl like Qiandao Lake. It has never failed to impressed the visitors with its breathtaking beauty. To travel from the West Lake in Hangzhou to Qiandao Lake, Shexian and Huangshan has become a hot tourist line.

Taiping Lake. An artificial deep water lake, Taiping Lake is situated between the Yellow Mountains and Mount Jiuhua. It extends 80 kilometers from east to west, which is roughly the same distance down the Li River from Guilin to Yangsuo, and covers an area of about 100 square kilometers. In addition to tour yachts, one can also take a black awning boat, a fishing boat or even a bamboo raft to enjoy the lake scene. The lake is clear and tranquil all the year round. The famous Peach Blossom Pool is located at the Wan Village on the lakeside. The famous Tang Dynasty poet Li bai once toured the lake and wrote a poem in appreciation of the hospitality of Wang Lun, his host. The poem is well recited today. Later, the villagers built a pavilion in memory of the great poet, which still stands. One scene in the TV series of the classical Chinese novel the Dream of the Red Mansion was shot here at the lakeside.

Vast as the lake is, scenic spots still abound, such as the group of isles in the lake known as the 18 Arhats and the Cave of Immortals on Jiaoshan Hill near the lake. Tourist facilities such as holiday resorts, amusement ground, shops and swimming grounds are open to holiday seekers. And there in nothing more relaxing than drifting in a raft or boat or going angling on the lake.

The Guniujiang Nature Reserve. Literally, Guniujiang means in Chinese an ox descending from the sky. It is so named because a big rock on the peak resembles a big ox that has just landed from the sky. Straddling Qimen and Shitai Counties, the reserve covers an area of 30 square kilometers, with the Guniujiang Peak, which is the highest peak, rising 1727.6 meters high. It is one of the nature reserves of forest and wild life in China as well as an ideal ground for making expedition trips.

The reserve is of complex geological structure, with numerous cliffs, peaks, rocks of grotesque shapes, falls, brooks and lakes. Sometimes, Buddhist halo with rainbow colors appears around the peaks, adding to the fascination of the mountain view. The natural vegetation is well preserved here, with distinct vertical distribution of plants. At the mountain top is growth of grass. Half way up the mountain are deciduous leaf trees and evergreen broadleaf trees. Rare species of trees and plants abound, such as Xiangguo tree, which is under priority state protection, large tracts of Yellow Mountain pine, Chinese catalpa, Wild Jujube tree, Nanmu wood, Qingqian willow, languo tree, Tenghuang sandalwood and cancer-resistant Sanjian fir as well as a dozen species of azalea.

The reserve is also a haven of wild animals where sika, sumen antelope, black muntjac, cloud leopard, macaque, short-tailed monkey, civet, otter, white cranes, pheasant with white neck and long tail, mandarin duck, pangolin and owls roam around.

The Qingliang Peak Nature Reserve. It straddles the border areas of Anhui and Zhejiang Provinces, with Qingliang Peak, which is the main peak, located in Shexian County. The reserve borders on Jixi County in the northwest and Lin'an county of Zhejiang Province in the northeast. Covering an area of 15 square kilometers, it is a major nature reserve and scenery ground in Anhui Province. Qingliang Peak is the main peak of the Tianmu Mountains, thrusting into the sky with a height of 1,780 meters. There are many enchanting scenic spots as well as falls and brooks on the hill. They stir up people's imagination of being in a fairy land.

The reserve is rich in vegetation, with over 400 species of woody plants in 85 families and over 1,000 species of herbal plants. The rare species of trees include East China yellow fir, red bean fir, sanjian fir, gold coin pine, China catalpa, magua wood, pearl yellow poplar, Yellow Mountain plum, etc. East China yellow fir is an endangered species of the Cretaceous period. There is now only one standing near the Cloud Valley Temple in the Yellow Mountains. Yet here in the reserve one finds large tracts of them. Arrow bamboo, which is the main diet of panda, is also found here. Rare animals such as Maoguan deer, zibet, golden cat, Sumen antelope, macaque and black muntjac wander freely in the reserve.

In addition to enjoying the beauty of the nature, visitors also have the opportunity to appreciate the distinctive local culture with its renowned architecture, carving, painting, epigraphy, lacquer making, calligraphy, pottery art, potted landscape, bamboo weaving as well as local opera and folk songs and dances. The architecture of the region, its economic development, medicine and folklore have become subjects of study, so have the philosophy of Daizhen, mathematics writing of Cheng Dawei and educational writings of Tao Xingzhi who were all natives of this region. The famous local teas such as Qimen black tea, Tunxi green tea, Yellow Mountain Maofeng tea and Taiping Houkui tea as well as Santan loquat, golden dates and local cuisine are favored by tourists. No one who has visited the Yellow Mountains leaves unimpressed by its fascination.

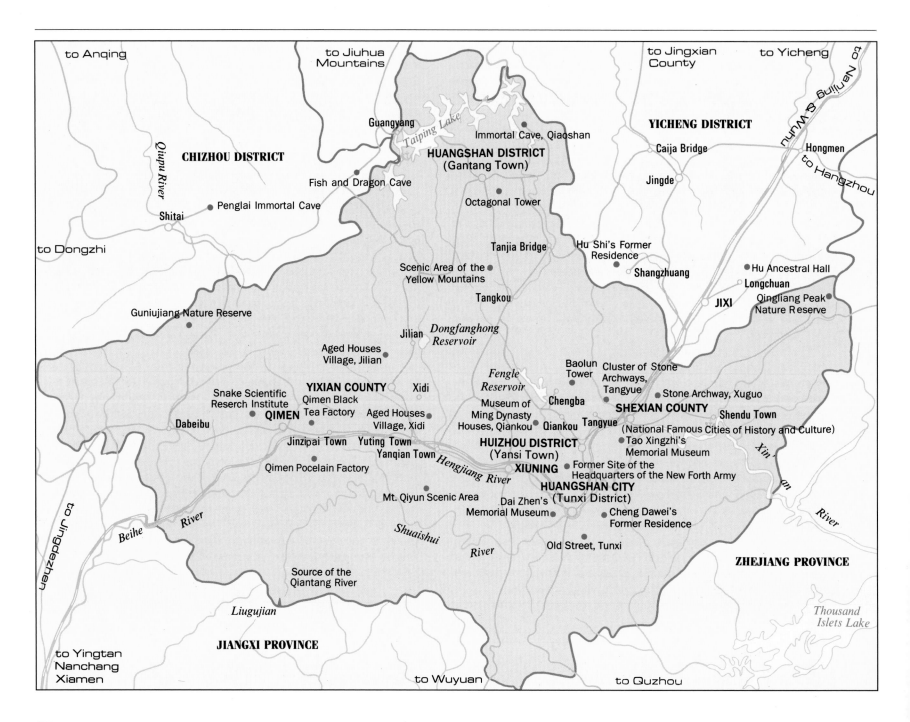

to Anqing

to Jiuhua
Mountains

to Jingxian
County

to Yicheng

to Nanjing & Wuhu

Guangyang

Taiping Lake

Immortal Cave, Qiaoshan

YICHENG DISTRICT

Caija Bridge

Hongmen

to Hangzhou

Qiupu River

CHIZHOU DISTRICT

HUANGSHAN DISTRICT
(Gantang Town)

Jingde

Fish and Dragon Cave

Octagonal Tower

Penglai Immortal Cave

Shitai

to Dongzhi

Tanjia Bridge

Hu Shi's Former
Residence

Hu Ancestral Hall

Scenic Area of the
Yellow Mountains

Shangzhuang

Longchuan

Tangkou

JIXI

Qingliang Peak
Nature Reserve

Guniujiang Nature Reserve

*Dongfanghong
Reservoir*

Jilian

Aged Houses
Village, Jilian

Baolun
Tower

Cluster of Stone
Archways,
Tangyue

YIXIAN COUNTY

Xidi

*Fengle
Reservoir*

Stone Archway, Xuguo

Snake Scientific
Reserch Institute

Qimen Black
Tea Factory

Chengba

SHEXIAN COUNTY

Shendu Town

QIMEN

Museum of
Ming Dynasty
Houses, Qiankou

Qiankou

Tangyue

(National Famous Cities of History and Culture)

Dabeibu

Aged Houses
Village, Xidi

Jinzipai Town

Yuting Town

HUIZHOU DISTRICT
(Yansi Town)

Tao Xingzhi's
Memorial Museum

Yanqian Town

Hengjiang River

Qimen Pocelain Factory

XIUNING

Former Site of the
Headquarters of the New Forth Army

HUANGSHAN CITY
(Tunxi District)

*Xin
An*

River

Mt. Qiyun Scenic Area

Dai Zhen's
Memorial Museum

Cheng Dawei's
Former Residence

Shuaishui

River

Old Street, Tunxi

ZHEJIANG PROVINCE

Beihe

River

to Jingdezhen

Source of the
Qiantang River

Liugujian

*Thousand
Islets Lake*

JIANGXI PROVINCE

to Yingtan
Nanchang
Xiamen

to Wuyuan

to Quzhou

106. "Lu Fu Tang"-Aged House in Yixian
County

107. Ox Stamach Pool in Hongcun
Village

108. Deep Lane
109. Well Terrace
110. Nanhu Lake in Hongcun Village

111. Stone Archway for Hu Wenguang in
     Xidi Village
112. Gild Balcony in Xidi Village
113. Bamboo Groves, Mukeng

FAMOUS HISTORICAL AND CULTURAL SITES IN SHEXIAN COUNTY

115. Stone Archway, Xuguo
116. Stone Archway with Eight
     Reinforcements

117. Garden of Stone Steles, Xin'an
118. A Bird's-eye View of the Cluster of
    Stone Archways, Tangyue

119. Taibai Tower—Build to Commemorate the Great Poet Li Bai
120. Memorial Museum of People's Educator Tao Xingzhi
121. Former Residence of the Landscape Painter Huang Binhong

122. Doushan Street—Aged Lane,Shexian
County
123. Wood Carvings
124. Stone Carvings

125. Brick Carvings
126. Song Dynasty Pagoda in the Changqing Temple

127. Hu Shi's Former Residence—
　　　Shangzhuang Village, Jixi
128. Hu Shi's Memorial Museum

THE XIN'AN RIVER

131. Fishing
132. Fishing Family
133. Old Commercial Port on the Xin'an River

134. Stone Archway at Tangmo with Inscription "Fellow Members of Imperial Academy"

135. Yansi Pagoda
136. Village with the Ming Dynasty
     Houses
137. Baolun Pavilion, Chengkan

SCENIC AREA AT MOUNTAIN CITY
OF TUNXI

138. Dragon Dance during the Festival,
Tunxi

139. Old Shopping Street, Tunxi.
140. Laofuchun Shop
141. Meigeyi Soy Sauce Workshop
142. Tongderen Chinese Medicine Shop

143. Red Lanterns Sale during the Festival
144. Lion Dance during the Lantern Festival
145. Walking on Stilts during the Lantern Party

146. Former Residence of the Great Ming Dynasty Mathematician Cheng Dawei
147. Memorial Museum of the Famous Qing Dynasty Philosopher Dai Zhen
148. Black Awning Boat on the Xin'an River

QIYUN MOUNTAIN SCENIC AREA
AT XIUNING COUNTY

149. A Bird's-eye View of the Aged Town

150. Cruising the Hengjiang River on
    Bamboo Raft
151. Aged Dengfeng Bridge

152. Clouds Roaming in the Qiyun
    Mountain.

153. Immortal's Cave Residence.
154. Stone Stele Forest at Yitianmen
155. Stone Inscription—"Longevity"

156. Xiaohutian
157. Purple Cloud Rock

158. Waterfall
159. Stone Stele for Tang Yin

160. Stone Sculpture of Zhou Cang
Leading a Horse

161. Qiyun Mountain in the Sunshine
162. Relief of Taoist Priest Zhang Ling Becoming An Immortal After Obtaining Heavenly Virtues

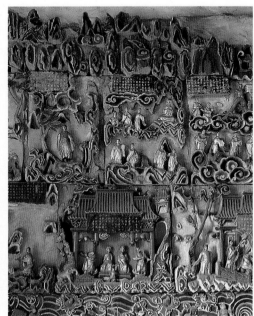

TAIPING LAKE SCENIC AREA

LOCAL SCENES AND CUSTOMS IN SOUTHERN ANHUI

165. Country in Autumn

166. Aged Waterwheel Drawing Water
167. Spring Circling the Mountain Village

171. Aged House
172. Old Man and His Birds

FAMOUS LOCAL PRODUCES OF THE YELLOW MOUNTAINS

173. Painting Anhui Ink Sticks with Golden Colour
174. Shexian Ink Slab
175. Anhui Ink Sticks

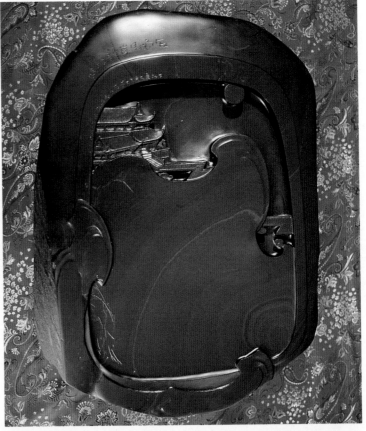

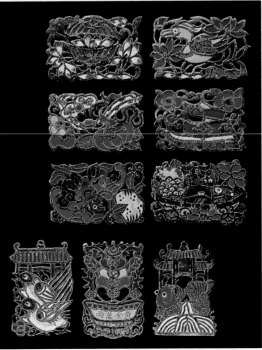

179. Ceramic, Qimen
180. Lacquerwares

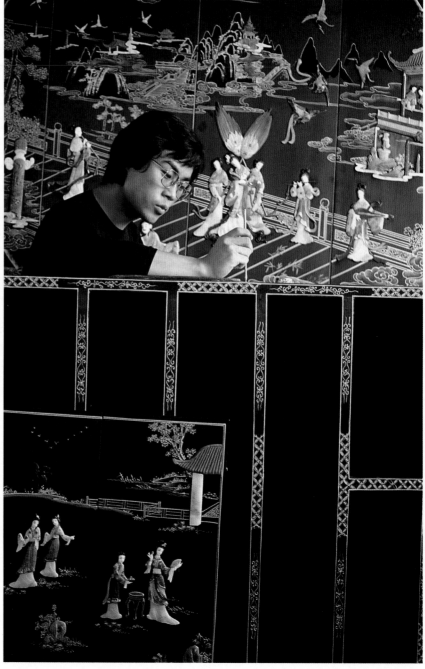

181. Bamboo Wares
182. Maofeng Tea of the Yellow
    Mountains
183. Ancient Compass, Wanan

ANHUI DISHES AND SNACKS

138

SERVICE FACILITIES

188. West Sea Hotel
189. Lobby of the West Sea Hotel·
190. Huaxi Hotel
   Huashan Guesthouse

191. Taoyuan Guesthouse
192. Yungu Shanzhuang Hotel
193. Swimming Pool at the Hot Spring

194 . North Sea Guesthouse
195 . Yupinglou Hotel

196. Airport of the Yellow Mountains
197. Air Hostess Is Serving the Guests

HUANGSHAN MOUNTAINS

Published by China Travel & Tourism Press
(A9 Jianguomennei Street, Beijing)
Printed by Tianshi Printing Company Ltd.
Distributed by China Travel & Tourism Press
First Edition 1991
ISBN 7—5032-0475-3/K · 112
005900